Garnishing
FOR THE
Beginner
by Harvey Rosen

*"Welcome To, **Garnishing For The Beginner**...
I've created this book especially for those who
doubt their ability to create distinctive and
beautiful garnishes. The easy-to-follow step-by-
step instructions and drawings will teach even a
beginner how to create a pleasing centerpiece or
plate decoration. For those of you that have some
experience in garnishing, this book may contain
some new ideas that you will want to add to your
garnishing library. I invite you to share some of
your favorite garnishes that you find particularly
pleasing. Send to Chef Harvey at the address below."*

Wishing You Joy At Your Table!

Chef Harvey

Published By:
International Culinary Consultants
P.O. Box 2202 Elberon Station
Elberon, New Jersey 07740 U.S.A.

Cyberspace Address:
E-mail: chefharvey@aol.com
Web Site: http://www.chef-harvey.com

Melon Whale

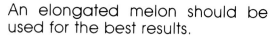

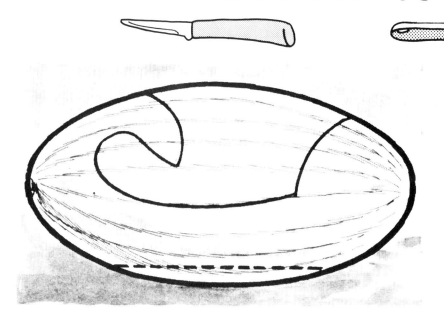

An elongated melon should be used for the best results.

To stabilize the whale cut a thin slice from the bottom of the melon. Draw the lines of the whale as shown.

Cut an X through the rind in the section that is to be discarded.
This will help prevent splitting of ripe watermelon.

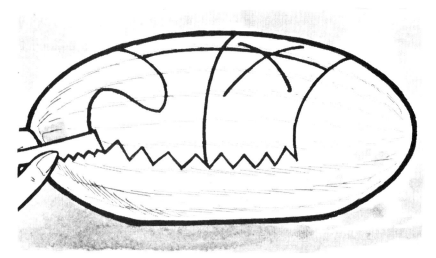

Use a v-shaped food decorating tool to make the zig zag edges along the side.
Use a sharp paring knife to cut the tail and head section.

Cut the top section in quarters to aid in the removal of the rind.
Use a small paring knife to carve the mouth and eyes.

Hollow the shell and fill it with melon balls or mixed fruit.

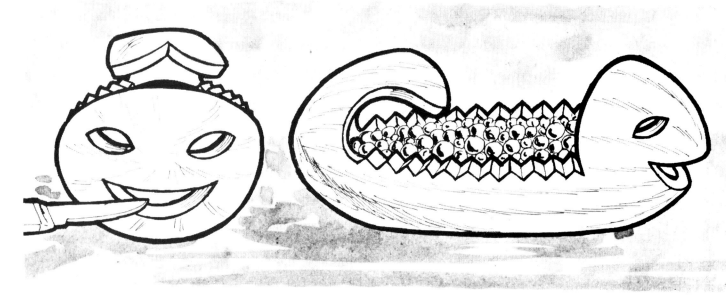

Melon Basket

For the best results, select a melon that is oval in shape.

To provide a stable base, cut a thin slice from the bottom of the melon.

Draw the lines of the basket on the melon before you start cutting.

Draw one line horizontally around the center of the melon.

Then draw the handle by drawing two lines a few inches apart at the top of the melon.

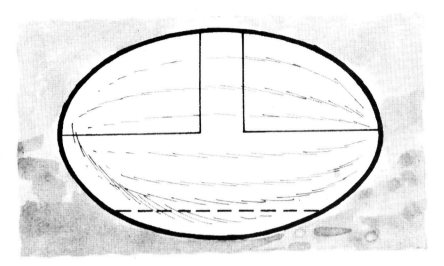

Cut an X through the rind in the sections to be discarded to reduce the chances of splitting.

Use a v-shaped food decorating tool to make the zig zag pattern along the edges.

Insert the point of the tool at least half way into the melon along the line that was just drawn.

Continue making v-shaped cuts along the line being sure they connect.

Be careful not to cut through the handle.

When the cutting is completed, lift the top quarter sections off carefully.

Use a knife to remove the pulp of the watermelon from the rind.

A melon ball scoop may be used to form balls to fill the basket.

Also, fruits such as grapes, cherries, strawberries, pineapple, and various melons may be used to fill the melon, if desired.

Decorate the handle with citrus slices, melon balls, and cherries attached with toothpicks to give the basket a professional touch.

Carved Rose

Holding the root end, make four connecting diagonal cuts into the side of the vegetable.

Carve a ring around the circumference behind the petals and remove the ring.

This forms the first row of petals.

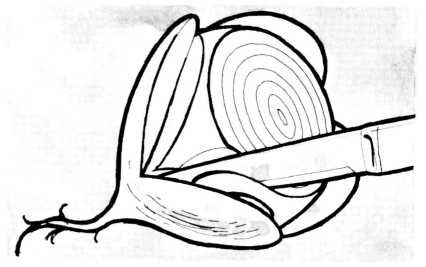

To make more petals simply repeat the same steps but make the diagonal cuts in between the previous row of petals to give a floral effect.

The number of rows depends upon the size of the vegetable.

Soak the roses in ice water to open the petals further.

Potato roses can be deep fried or baked.

Roses can be made ahead of time and stored in ice water in the refrigerator until serving.

−Onion Mum−

Select a large, tall, white or red onion for this garnish.
Try to select an onion with a single growth.

Use a paring knife to make cuts half way into the onion, 3/4 of the way to the root end.

Place a toothpick into the root end and immerse in hot water for a few minutes to remove the odor.
Then soak in ice water to open the petals further.

White onion mums can be colored with food coloring to enhance the appearance.

Stuffed Potatoes

Use a twin curl cutter to hollow the center of a baking potato.
Insert the point of the tool into the end of the potato and attach the handle to the end of the shaft.
Press lightly and turn the tool clockwise.

When the double ring appears at the other end, remove the handle and slide the shaft through.

Remove the solid curls from the center by turning them clockwise. Stuff the hollowed potato shell with cheese, chopped meat, sausage or other food.

Wrap the potato in saran wrap for a microwave oven or aluminum foil for a conventional oven and bake.

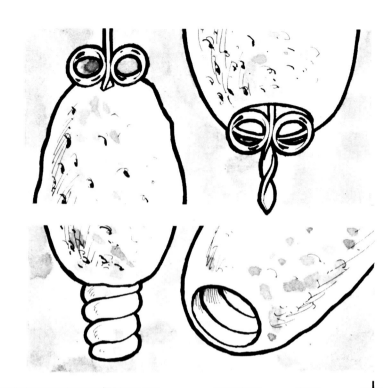

STUFFED POTATO RECIPE
4 med. baking potatoes
1 egg
1 package onion soup mix
1 lb. chopped beef
3 tbsp. barbecue sauce

Bake the hollowed pototoes 10 minutes in a microwave oven on high or 45 minutes in a conventional oven at 350°F.

Let stand while preparing the following:
Beat the egg with a fork, add the package of onion soup mix, mix well; add the chopped beef and the barbecue sauce to the egg and soup mixture. Fill the pre-cooked potatoes with this filling and then micro-cook them another 5-8 minutes or bake them for another 15 minutes.

Stuffed Cucumbers

Cut a large cucumber in half and work on each half separately.

The skin of the cucumber may be scored if desired.

Hollow the soft center of the cucumber with an apple corer or a twin curl cutter.
Insert the point of the twin curl and attach the key to the end of the shaft.

Press lightly and turn the tool clockwise, removing the soft section as you go.
Be sure to pierce the end of the cucumber.
Stuff the hollow shell with mixtures of chopped pickle, salmon or chives with cream cheese.
Place in the refrigerator until firm and then cut into slices.
The cucumber shell can also be stuffed with a carrot and cut into slices.

Candy Cane Vegetables

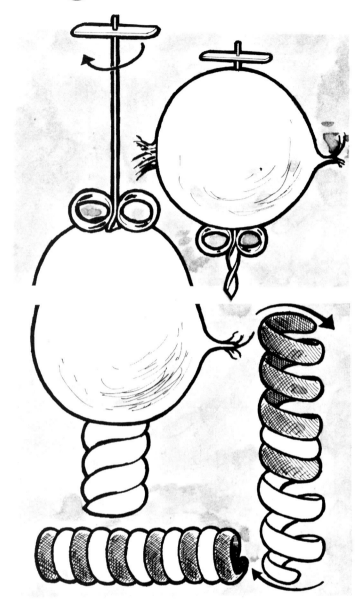

Attach the handle to the end of the shaft of the tool and insert the point of the tool into the center of the vegetable.

When using beets or turnips, select those that are short and wide and insert the tool through the side, not the root end.

Press lightly and turn the tool clockwise.
Continue turning until the double rings cut through the other end of the vegetable.

Remove the handle and slide the shaft out the bottom.
To remove the curls from the vegetable, turn them clockwise; do not pull them.

The curls are used to make the candy cane vegetables and the hollowed section may be used to create stuffed vegetables.

To separate the two curls, turn them in opposite directions.
Intertwine curls from beets, carrots, turnips, and potatoes to produce candy cane vegetables.
Beet, turnip, and carrot curls may be simmered in lightly salted water for 8-10 minutes or pickled.

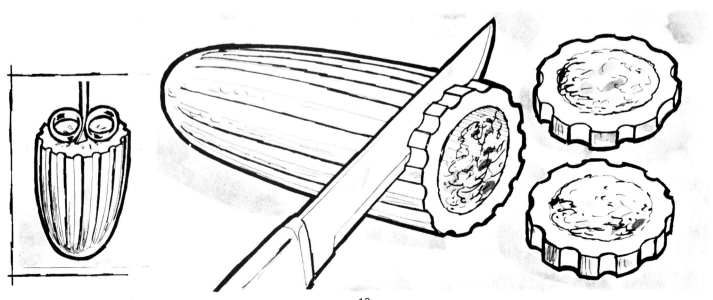

Spiral Vegetables

The vegetable should be at room temperature to prevent splitting.

Use a knife or a corrugated garnishing tool to cut the vegetable into a cylinder shape.

Insert the screw of the spiral slicer into the center of the top of the vegetable.

Place your finger into the hole and turn the tool clockwise.

As you turn the tool the screw will work its way through the vegetable and carve a spiral design.

Attach the ends of the spiral together with a toothpick.

The potato spiral can be fried.

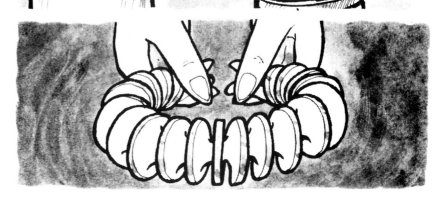

Potato Chips

Potato chips, home fries, or cottage fries can be made from the spiral potato by cutting with a paring knife down the screw hole and making a single cut outward.

Separate the slices and fry to a golden brown.

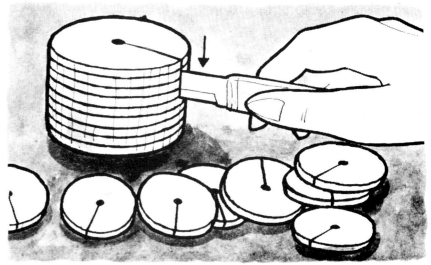

Strip Tomato Rose

With a sharp paring knife peel the skin from a firm unblemished tomato.
Start at the stem end and continue peeling in one continuous strip 3/4 inch wide.
Remove as much flesh from the strip as possible.

Form a rose by rolling the strip in a tight coil, keeping the stem end to the outside.
Hold the rose together with a toothpick.

Tomato Surprise

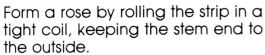

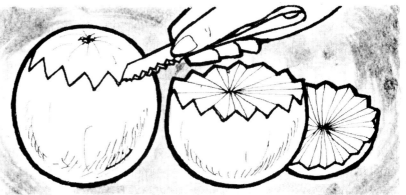

Select a large ripe tomato for this garnish.
Use a v-shaped food decorator or a sharp paring knife to form a zig-zag cut around the stem end.
Remove the top section and hollow out the tomato to make a shell.

Fill the shell with tuna, egg or chicken salad, cottage cheese, cooked carrots or peas.
Add a radish rose or an olive to complete the garnish.